The Poem Forest

Poet W. S. Merwin and the Palm Tree Forest
He Grew from Scratch

Carrie Fountain

illustrated by Chris Turnham

CANDLEWICK PRESS

EVER SINCE he was a child, William Stanley loved wild places: the trees and the bugs and the rich smell of the earth and the sounds of birds, and the great, big feeling of silence on top of it all.

William Stanley didn't live in the wilderness, not at all. William Stanley lived in a town like any other town, where the wild parts had been straightened out and turned into roads and lawns and driveways.

Outside his town, that place had also been turned into a town, and so on and so on for a long distance. William Stanley sometimes had bad dreams that the whole world might become like that, all the wild parts straightened out and paved over and lost forever.

In summer, William Stanley went with his family to a cabin in the woods. Traveling there, he liked to watch the straight lines of towns disappear and the sky get wider and the trees get untidy until it was wild all around.

He felt at home in the wilderness, where trees grew where their seeds
had fallen and the noises were wild noises and birds lived the way birds
had always lived, in trees and in the sky.

As he grew up, William Stanley also learned that he loved to write poems. For William Stanley, writing poetry was like visiting a wild place—a surprising place always just exactly itself, language growing wherever it pleased.

It couldn't be straightened out.

He went to school and studied and read books and wrote poems.
He became a man and traveled and lived all over. Still, he always felt a
little out of place in the straightened-out world of towns and cities.

He had a hunch he'd find his wilderness in Hawaii, where many places were still wild. A hunch is like a seed for a thought you haven't had yet.

William Stanley knew he'd have to plant the seed to find out what it would grow into.

So William Stanley moved to Hawaii, where he looked all over the island of Maui for a perfect spot, waiting for the wild place inside himself—the place where his poems came from—to speak up, to say, *Yes. This is the spot.*

He was surprised when he found that his perfect wild spot wasn't perfect or wild at all. It was wounded. It had been stripped of all its rich, dark soil. "Sure you want that spot?" lots of people asked. They told him nothing would grow there.

The word some people used to describe it was *wasteland*.

But when William Stanley stood on the wounded ground, the wild place inside him spoke up. He heard the birds above and could feel the future that would grow there, a future thick with trees.

He'd found a straightened-out place longing to grow wild.

He had a hunch. "Yes, thanks," William Stanley said. "This is the spot."

The very first day, William Stanley dug a hole in the ground and planted a tree. Putting the delicate roots into the earth was a way of promising he meant what he'd said. *Yes, thanks. This is the spot.*

Many people believed in William Stanley's promise. With friends and family, he built a small, quiet house on the land. He learned that the trees that grew best there were palm trees. And so every day during the rainy season, William Stanley planted at least one palm tree. Every day, a tree.

Each year, the soil became richer and the palms grew taller and more wild. The wounded earth healed.

Soon, there wasn't a straightened-out
thing anywhere.

As his trees grew, William Stanley's poems grew, too. People around the world read William Stanley's poems, and many people found they helped them find the rich, dark soil of their own lives. He won many awards and even served as Poet Laureate of the United States.

But there was always room for surprises. One thing William Stanley didn't know when he started planting is that there are more than three thousand species of palm trees.

He learned that some of the world's palm trees are in danger of being the last of their kind because the places where they grow wild are being straightened out into towns or, worse, turned into wastelands.

And so William Stanley made a promise to the almost-lost palms of the world. He would find them and bring them from all over and give them a home in his forest.

Trees arrived from all over the world. William Stanley found a place for each one.

William Stanley and his wife Paula were happy in the quiet house in what had become the middle of the forest they'd grown. Over many, many years, their promises had grown tall all around them.

When he got very old, William Stanley found he had one more promise to keep. He and Paula wanted to make sure someone would be there after they were gone, to plant the seeds and care for the palms and to keep the promise they'd made to the earth all those years ago.

And so they gave their forest away.

They gave the land to a conservancy. Now, because of the Merwin Conservancy, the soil will never again be wounded and there will always be someone there to plant a tree every day during the rainy season.

The wild place William Stanley and Paula grew over all those years, the forest they made of love and promises and poems and silence and rain, will never stop growing.

This wild place will never be straightened out.

AUTHOR'S NOTE

William Stanley Merwin, who wrote as W. S. Merwin, was born in 1927 in New York City and grew up in Union City, New Jersey, and Scranton, Pennsylvania. His father was a Presbyterian minister, and William started writing hymns, or songs, when he was only five years old. He thought his hymns were pretty good, and was disappointed when they weren't used in his father's church. Still, his long career as a writer had begun.

In high school, a Spanish teacher recognized William's passion and encouraged his poetry writing. He also introduced William to the art of translating other people's poems. Writing and translating poetry would become William's life work.

William's parents couldn't afford to send him to college, but he was given a scholarship to study at Princeton University, where he supported himself by waiting tables on campus. After college, he wrote poems, translated poetry, and traveled and lived all over the world. In 1976, he went to Hawaii to study Zen Buddhism with a special teacher. There he met the poet and activist Dana Naone, with whom he began planting trees and with whose help he built the sustainable house. Later, he met his wife Paula, and the two lived together in the palm forest for the rest of their lives.

William wrote that in the local record books, the land he bought on Maui "was—and still is—described as a wasteland, with a hand-scrawled note below it saying 'nothing will grow here.'" Over the course of thirty-five years, working together day by day, William and Paula Merwin planted nearly three thousand palm trees there, living at the center of their forest in a house that uses rainwater and solar energy. "In gardening," William once wrote, "as my wife and I go about it here, what are called concerns—for ecology and the environment, for example—merge inevitably with work done every day, within sight of the house, with our own hands, and the concerns remain intimate and familiar rather than far away." Their commitment to the simple act of planting transformed the so-called wasteland into one of the most comprehensive palm forests on planet Earth.

William's long commitment to writing left the world with a great wealth of poems, and his poetry was celebrated with many awards. Over his lifetime, he won two Pulitzer Prizes and the National Book Award. He was named Poet Laureate of the United States in 2010 and traveled to Washington, DC, to meet with President Obama at the White House.

William wrote poems and planted trees as a daily practice, and his example of daily work and long commitments continues to inspire generations of poets and ecologists. In 2010, William and Paula established the Merwin Conservancy, which will protect and grow the palm forest in perpetuity.

William Stanley Merwin died on March 15, 2019. Though he didn't have a chance to see it, he knew the book you're holding in your hands would be published.

PALM

The palm is in no hurry
to be different
and it grows slowly
it knows how to be a palm
when it was a seed it knew
how to be a palm seed
when it was a flower
it knew how to be
the flower of a palm
when it was a palm it grew
slowly
and without eyes
in a salt wind

—W. S. Merwin
from *Opening the Hand*

For Olive and Judah
CF

For Kirsten
CT

Text copyright © 2022 by Carrie Fountain
Illustrations copyright © 2022 by Chris Turnham

The poem "Palm" at the end of this book was first published in *Opening the Hand*.
Copyright © 1983 by W. S. Merwin, used here by permission of The Wylie Agency LLC

First edition 2022

Library of Congress Catalog Card Number pending
ISBN 978-1-5362-1126-9

22 23 24 25 26 27 APS 10 9 8 7 6 5 4 3 2 1

Printed in Humen, Dongguan, China

This book was typeset in Archer.
The illustrations were created digitally.

Candlewick Press
99 Dover Street
Somerville, Massachusetts 02144

www.candlewick.com